Introducti

Good-looking and beautifully-garnished fo
decorations, created in the main from fruit
thing you serve extra special. Once you ge
and twirling, you should gain confidence, b
perfect.

Merehurst Limited
Ferry House, 51-57 Lacy Road,
Putney, London SW15 1PR

Copyright © Gräfe und Unzer GmbH
1993, Munich

ISBN 1 874567 11 5

Designed by Clive Dorman & Co.
Printed in Italy by G. Canale & C.S.p.A

Distributed in the UK by
J.B. Fairfax Press Limited,
9 Trinity Centre, Park Farm,
Wellingborough, Northants NN8 6ZB

Distributed in Australia by
J.B. Fairfax Press Pty Ltd,
80 McLachlan Avenue,
Rushcutters Bay,
Sydney, NSW 2011

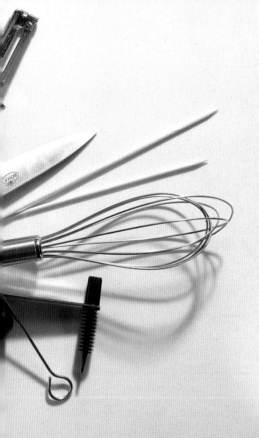

Tomato Rose

An elegant and classic decoration, perfect for all savoury dishes.

Preparation time: about 5 minutes

FOR ONE TOMATO ROSE
1 large firm tomato, with a smooth, deep
red skin

EQUIPMENT
1 small and very sharp kitchen knife and/or
sharp vegetable peeler

1 Wash tomato thoroughly and wipe dry.
Avoid tomatoes with blemishes on the
skin as this will spoil the appearance of the
rose.

2 Carefully remove stalk, then make a
small slit in the same spot.

3 Beginning at the slit, start peeling the
tomato like an apple with knife or
vegetable peeler. Work slowly and cut skin
as thinly as possible without allowing it to
break. If skin is too thick, it will be hard to roll.

4 With skin side out, roll one end of the
peel round a finger. Lift off and
continue to roll until you have what looks like
a rosebud. The appearance of the rose is
sometimes more attractive if it is turned
upside down.

VARIATION
Instead of a tomato, use the peel of a
lemon, orange or lime. You can also make
an apple peel rose but it must be sprinkled
with lemon juice to avoid browning.

TIP
The rose is more for aesthetics than eating,
but the remaining skinned tomato can be
used for cooking or added to salads.

Tomato Rose

Courgette (Zucchini) Concertina

Quick to do and very impressive.

Preparation time: about 20 minutes

FOR 1 CONCERTINA
1 slender courgette (zucchini)
Salt
Freshly milled pepper
Juice of ½ lemon
1 tablespoon virgin olive oil

EQUIPMENT
1 small sharp kitchen knife
1 long wooden or metal skewer

1 Choose courgette (zucchini) which is straight and no thicker than 4cm/1¾ in diameter. This makes cutting easier and also helps to prevent concertina from breaking.

2 Wash courgette (zucchini) thoroughly, then top and tail with knife.

3 Starting at one end, carefully push skewer lengthwise through the centre of courgette (zucchini), using a twisting action. Holding top of the skewer with one hand, cut and turn the courgette (zucchini) simultaneously with the other hand, making the slices as even as possible.

4 Continue until the whole courgette (zucchini) has been cut, then gently ease out skewer.

5 Open out the concertina on a plate, sprinkle with salt, pepper and lemon juice and leave for 15 minutes so that excess juices from courgette (zucchini) are drawn out. This makes it less brittle and easier to handle.

6 Gently lift concertina on to absorbent kitchen paper and leave to drain before using to garnish cold, savoury dishes.

VARIATION
Instead of courgette (zucchini), use white radish (Japanese daikon). For a very pretty effect, twist together two spirals of green and yellow courgette (zucchini).

Courgette (Zucchini) Concertina

Radish Crown

An attractive garnish which makes a pleasant change
from usual vandyke radish.

Preparation time: about 30 minutes

FOR 10 CROWNS
10 radishes

EQUIPMENT
1 small sharp kitchen knife
1 small bowl

1 Remove and discard radish leaves if necessary. Top and tail each radish. Cut a thin sliver off the base of each so that it stands upright without toppling over.

2 Using a sharp knife, cut a small wedge out of the top of radish.

3 Repeat twice more to give you what looks like a six-pointed star.

4 Starting at the top, make six petals by cutting two-thirds of the way down each radish, working between points of star as shown in the picture. Repeat with remaining radishes.

5 Drop radishes into a bowl of iced-cold water and chill for 10 minutes. This makes the petals open out and also crispens the radishes. Do not leave them to soak as they might lose both taste and colour.

VARIATIONS
To make chrysanthemum radishes, cut a sliver off the base of each so that they stand up straight. Starting at the top, cut downwards into thin slices. Give radishes a quarter turn and cut downwards again as before, taking care not to slice through bases. Drop radishes into bowl of iced-cold water, leave for 2 minutes then drain. For picture, see inside of back cover.

Radish Crown

Cucumber Variations

Cucumber makes a versatile garnish for cold savoury dishes.

Preparation time: about 15 minutes

FOR TWO FANS AND ONE BUNDLE
1 medium cucumber

EQUIPMENT
1 kitchen knife
1 chopping board

1 Wash cucumber thoroughly and wipe dry with absorbent kitchen paper. Cut cucumber into 3 pieces.

2 Cut each piece in half lengthwise. Place on board, cut sides down.

3 To make fan with tail end of cucumber, cut into thin slices lengthwise, almost to top, and open out.

4 To make a short, curvy fan, cut second portion of cucumber into thin parallel slices widthwise as shown on top right of picture. Make sure you don't cut right through to the top edge so that they are joined along the top. Spread out as shown on the top left of picture.

5 To make cucumber bundle, cut last portion of cucumber lengthwise into long, thinnish slices.

6 Lay each slice down flat and make nicks, fairly close together, from outside edge to centre cutting about half-way down. Do not cut right through from one side to the other, or bundle will fall apart.

7 Roll up and hold in place with cocktail stick.

VARIATION
Use young and small courgettes (zucchini) instead of cucumber.

Cucumber Variations

Meat Platter

Serves 6

A selection of bought meats turns into something special with some garnishes.

Preparation time: about 45 minutes

775g (1lb 8oz) sliced, cooked meats

GARNISH
Courgette (zucchini) Concertina, pages 6-7
Radish Crowns, pages 8-9
Cucumber Fans, pages 10-11
Tomato Roses, pages 4-5
Cucumber Bundle, pages 10-11

DRESSING
1 packet fresh mixed herbs
1 egg yolk
15ml (3tsp) Continental mustard
Salt to taste
Freshly milled pepper to taste
Juice of ½ lemon
100ml (3½ fl oz/½ cup) sunflower or corn oil
15ml (3tsp) single cream

1 Arrange the meats around the outside of a large plate.

2 Arrange the courgette (zucchini) concertina, radish crowns, tomato rose and cucumber fans on the cooked meats.

3 To make dressing: wash and dry herbs and coarsely chop. Spoon into blender. Add the egg yolk, mustard, salt, pepper, lemon juice, oil and cream. Blend until smooth and pour into a small bowl.

4 Arrange the bowl in the centre of the serving plate. Add a cucumber bundle and a radish crown and serve at once.

Spring Onion (Green Shallot) Tassels

An impressive garnish which is easy to prepare.

Preparation time: about 30 minutes

FOR ONE TASSEL
1 thick spring onion (green shallot) or very young slender leek

EQUIPMENT
1 small vegetable knife
1 chopping board
1 bowl

1 Wash spring onion (green shallot) or leek thoroughly under cold running water.

2 Top and tail spring onion (green shallot) or leek, leaving on a generous length of green leaf. Put spring onion (green shallot) or leek on to chopping board.

3 Using the knife, slit the green part of the spring onion (green shallot) or leek just up to the white bulb. Do this several times to make fairly narrow strips. Repeat the splitting, first giving the spring onion (green shallot) or leek a quarter turn.

4 Soak spring onion (green shallot) or leek in cold water for 20 minutes until green leaves curl.

5 Remove from water and shake dry.

TIP
Spring leeks are perfect for tassels as they are usually tender and clean.

Spring Onion (Green Shallot) Tassels

Ways with Lemons

A fish dish would not be the same without a beautiful lemon garnish.

Preparation time: about 10 minutes

FOR 8 LOOPS AND 2-3 BUTTERFLIES
2 medium lemons

EQUIPMENT
1 small vegetable knife
1 chopping board

1 Choose firm, bright yellow lemons with unblemished skin.

2 Thoroughly wash and dry lemons.

3 For loops, halve one lemon lengthwise, then cut each half into 4 segments.

4 Gently cut flesh away from each segment, leaving it joined at the top by about 1cm/½ in. Carefully ease skin away from flesh then fold skin under flesh segment to form a loop. Repeat with remaining segments. See top right of picture.

5 For butterflies, cut off top and bottom of lemon then slice fruit thinly into a spiral, following method used for courgette (zucchini) concertina on pages 6-7, but without using a skewer.

6 Cut spiral into 2 or 3 pieces, depending on size of lemon, and twist into butterfly shapes as shown on bottom right of picture.

Ways with Lemons

Stuffed Eggs

*Attractively garnished, stuffed eggs make an appealing
centrepiece for any buffet table.*

Preparation time: about 30 minutes

FOR 12 EGG HALVES
6 eggs
1 tablespoon crème fraîche
Salt to taste
Freshly milled pepper to taste
2 radishes
1 packet fresh parsley
1 tablespoon tomato ketchup
4 sprigs of fresh dill
60g (2oz) cooked peeled prawns
2 teaspoons mock caviar or fish roe
small pickled red or green peppers
    (capsicums), drained
kiwi fruit

EQUIPMENT
1 kitchen knife
1 chopping board
3 small bowls
Icing bag fitted with star-shaped tube
1 hand whisk

1 Cook eggs in boiling water for 9
minutes. Drain, cover with cold water
and leave for 15 minutes. Drain again and
shell. Halve each egg lengthwise and spoon
yolks into a bowl. Mash finely. Cut a thin
sliver off the base of each egg white half to
stop it tilting over to one side.

2 Add crème fraîche to yolks and mix in
well. Season with salt and pepper.
Spoon one-third of the mixture into icing
bag and pipe into 4 egg white halves.

3 Top and tail radishes. Wash and dry
then cut into thin slices. Arrange in rings
on top of the 4 filled egg halves. Add a sprig
of parsley to centre of each.

4 Divide remaining egg mixture between
the two bowls. Add tomato ketchup to
one and mix in well. Chop remaining parsley. Add to egg mixture in second bowl,
working it in well.

5 Spoon or pipe the tomato-coloured yolk
mixture into 4 egg white halves. Repeat
with parsley-flavoured yolks, using up
remaining 4 whites. Wash dill and gently
wipe dry with absorbent kitchen paper.
Garnish parsley egg halves with prawns,
caviar and dill.

6 Garnish tomato egg halves with whole
chillies and half a peeled slice of kiwi
fruit.

Stuffed Eggs

Apple Chevrons

With a little practice you will be able to prepare this elegant garnish in minutes.

Preparation time: about 15 minutes

FOR 4 CHEVRONS
1 red apple
Juice of ½ lemon

EQUIPMENT
1 very sharp kitchen knife
Chopping board

1 Use shiny, red apples which are firm and unblemished.

2 Wash apples and wipe dry with absorbent kitchen paper. Cut into quarters. Top and tail to remove any hard pieces.

3 Remove core from each apple quarter, cutting across flesh to make flat surface which, when apple quarter is turned over, will stand securely.

4 Place quarter of apple on chopping board with skin side facing uppermost and cut a small V-shaped wedge from centre. Reserve.

5 Continue to cut out slender, but increasingly larger, V-shaped wedges from apple quarter as shown in picture. Aim to cut out four wedges in total.

6 Sprinkle flesh with lemon juice to prevent browning. Re-assemble wedges to form a feather or chevron design. Separate them out a little as shown on left of picture.

Apple Chevrons

Cheese Platter

Serves 6

Preparation time: about 1 hour

FOR CHEESE PLATTER
4 different kinds of cheese such as Gruyère,
Emmental, Gouda, Cheddar, Jarlsberg,
Brie or Camembert.

CHEESE CREAM
125g (4oz) fromage frais
60g (2oz) full fat soft cheese
2 tablespoons whipping cream or thick
soured cream
Salt and freshly milled pepper to taste

GARNISH
1 Spring Onion (Green Shallot) Tassel, see
page 14-15
3 or 4 Stuffed Egg halves, see pages 18-19
2 radishes
Sprigs fresh parsley
2 Tomato Roses, see pages 4-5
1 Apple Chevron, see pages 20-21

1 Allow cheeses to come to room
temperature.

2 Prepare cheese cream. Mix fromage
frais with soft cheese, cream, salt and
pepper. Spoon mixture into a small bowl.

3 Stand cheese cream in the centre of a
large platter and surround with sliced
cheeses as shown in picture. Place spring
onion (green shallot) tassel in centre of
cheese cream. Top egg halves with rings of
sliced radishes and parsley. Add tomato
roses and garnish with parsley. Add apple
chevron to platter.

4 Serve with crisp rolls or assorted breads.

Orange Shapes

A colourful decoration for both sweet or savoury dishes.

Preparation time: about 10 minutes

MAKES 4-5 KNOTS AND 2 TWISTS
2 medium oranges, preferably seedless

EQUIPMENT
1 medium kitchen knife
1 chopping board

1 Choose thin-skinned and unblemished oranges. If need be, buy 3 or 4 smaller oranges if they are the right kind.

2 Rub oranges clean under cold running water. Wipe dry, then cut a thin slice off top and bottom of each piece of fruit.

3 For knots, cut one orange into 5mm/¼ in thick slices. Make a nick through skin. Cut flesh away from peel three-quarters of the way round each slice.

4 Tie peel carefully into a loose knot and rest on orange flesh, see bottom right of picture. Use to decorate drinks and desserts or use as a garnish for fish dishes.

5 To make orange twists, prepare oranges as in step 2.

6 Cut orange into slices, then slit each slice from centre to outside edge.

7 Twist one slice into an S-shape, then twist second slice over the top to form a double twist.

TIP
If orange flesh breaks up when preparing the orange knots, cut thicker slices.

Orange Shapes

Chocolate Magic

*Chocolate-coated fruits and leaves are just a few of the tempting ways
of using chocolate as a decoration.*

Preparation time: about 30 minutes

TO COVER 10 LEAVES AND 10 STRAWBERRIES
155 g (5oz) plain (dark) chocolate
10 rose or fresh bay leaves (laurel leaves)
10 medium-sized strawberries

EQUIPMENT
1 small saucepan
1 medium bowl
1 tablespoon
1 fork

1 Break up chocolate and melt in bowl set over pan of gently simmering water. Stir from time to time ensuring no water comes into direct contact with the chocolate.

2 Carefully wash and dry rose or bay leaves. Using a pastry brush, cover bases of leaves with melted chocolate.

3 Carefully transfer leaves to a piece of plastic wrap or foil and leave to dry in cool place. When chocolate has completely set, gently peel away leaves. Use chocolate leaves for decorating gâteaux, ice creams, sorbets, mousses and pastries.

4 To make chocolate-covered strawberries, choose firm, top quality fruit.

5 Leave stalks in place, then gently wash and dry each strawberry. Using a fork, dip fruit into melted chocolate until well coated. Dry as leaves in step 3.

TIP
Instead of strawberries, use walnut or pecan nut halves.

Chocolate Magic

Feathered Designs

A classic garnish for desserts, much used by top chefs.

Preparation time: about 30 minutes

FOR 4 PLATES

500g (1lb) ripe apricots
220g (7oz) icing sugar, sifted
220g (7oz) fresh or frozen raspberries
2 teaspoons raspberry or apricot liqueur

EQUIPMENT

1 small knife
1 piping bag made from non-stick baking
   paper
1 wooden skewer or cocktail stick

1 To peel apricots, put into bowl and cover with boiling water. Leave to stand for 5 minutes. Drain and rinse under cold water then peel off skins. Halve apricots, remove stones and put flesh into blender or food processor with half the icing sugar. Blend to a smooth purèe. Spoon into clean bowl.

2 Gently wash raspberries (this is not necessary if frozen raspberries are being used) and blend to a smooth purée with remaining sugar and liqueur. Sieve.

3 Cover dessert plates evenly with apricot sauce, tilting them a little to ensure sauce completely covers centres of plates.

4 Transfer raspberry purèe to icing bag and pipe rings of raspberry mixture through tiny hole in tip of piping bag on top of apricot sauce, spacing lines out evenly and referring to picture for guidance.

5 Draw wooden skewer or cocktail stick in lines from centre of plate to outside edge. Reverse procedure, working from outside edge to centre to make snowflake design, see bottom right of picture.

Feathered Designs

Melon Vandyke

*An attractive way of presenting melon, especially when filled
with a colourful fruit salad.*

Preparation time: about 15 minutes

FOR 2 MELON BASKETS
1 medium Honeydew melon

FILLING
Fresh mixed fruit salad or sorbet
Mint leaves for decoration

EQUIPMENT
1 sharp kitchen knife
1 chopping board
1 tablespoon

1 When choosing a melon, press it gently on the top. If ripe, it will yield slightly to pressure and will have a lovely fragrant smell. Avoid melons which are hard and underripe.

2 Wash and dry melon, put on to chopping board then cut a thin slice away from top and bottom so that the halves will stand upright without tilting.

3 Place melon on its side and cut a deep vandyke pattern through the skin and flesh, slowly turning the fruit all the time and trying to keep cuts as even as possible.

4 Separate melon by carefully twisting and pulling two halves apart. Remove seeds with spoon.

5 Fill melon shell with lightly chilled fruit salad or scoops of sorbet. To serve, spoon fruit salad or sorbet and melon flesh on to plates and decorate with mint leaves.

Melon Vandyke

Dessert Spectacular

A magnificent array of mouth-watering sweets.

Preparation time: about 1¼ hours

½ Vandyke Melon, see pages 30-31, filled
with 5 or 6 scoops of assorted ice cream
or sorbet. Choose complimentary flavours,
but avoid peppermint which can be over-
powering.
Several chocolate-covered leaves, see
   pages 26-27
Chocolate-covered grapes, cherries and
   strawberries, see pages 26-27
1 orange knot, see pages 24-25
1 orange twist, see pages 24-25
1 plate feathered with apricot and raspberry purée, see pages 28-29

1 Stand the filled melon half on the left of
a large oval platter.

2 Add chocolate-covered leaves and
fruit and orange knots to platter as
shown in picture.

3 Top plate with feathered design with a
selection of chocolate-covered fruits,
some cut in half.

TIP
Dip fruits and leaves into the apricot and
raspberry purèe before eating.
Scoop ice cream, sorbet and melon flesh on
to plates before serving.

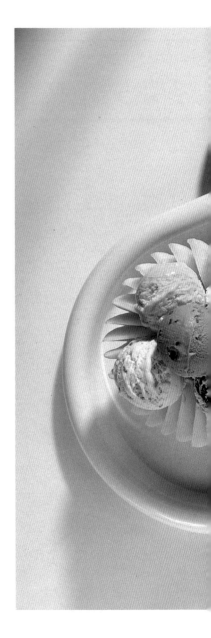

...and there's more!

Once you've mastered the basic techniques explained in the book, experiment with different fruits and vegetables. And keep practising. The more you do, the quicker and more professional your garnishes will be.

1 Courgettes work well instead of cucumbers for making fans. Follow the instructions on page 11. Use to garnish grilled meat and pasta dishes.

2 These colourful variations on a tomato rose are made with orange and lemon rind. Use to garnish fish or puddings like meringues and fruit salad.

3 Cut two similar-sized courgettes – one yellow and one green – into spirals as explained on page 6 and twist together for a two-tone effect.

4 The cucumber bundle illustrated on page 11 can be made with courgette and a large radish cut in a criss-cross pattern gives a similar effect.